Orthodoxy and Heresy:

Where to Draw the Line

Orthodoxy and Heresy:

Where to Draw the Line

By Joel Parkinson

Alliance Christian Center
670 West Main Street
Alliance, OH 44601

Companion Press
167 Walnut Bottom Road
P.O. Box 310
Shippensburg, PA 17257-0310

ISBN 1-56043-487-2

For Worldwide Distribution
Printed in the U.S.A.

Contents

Preface

Preface

Etymologically, orthodoxy means right belief. In this sense, to say that a doctrine is orthodox is simply to say that it is correct or true. Yet the word has also been applied to people as well as to specific doctrines. We speak of Christians and churches as being orthodox. This can hardly mean that such persons or groups of persons are correct in everything that they believe. No man short of the Lord Jesus Christ is perfect in faith. So apparently orthodoxy has come to mean something somewhat different than its strict etymological meaning when applied to the people of God. Traditionally, it seems to mean that those who are orthodox are sound in their beliefs about the central or essential truths of Christianity. The task is to determine what these beliefs are.

The present book presents a specific definition for the people-oriented meaning of orthodoxy followed by a discussion of the truths entailed in that meaning. I have chosen to simply state the definition, follow it to its logical conclusions and then examine the results in light of biblical truth. I have not attempted to buttress the definition itself with historical and philosophical arguments. These would be empty apart from the authority of the Bible (which does not use the word orthodoxy) and would merely add needless boredom to the text. Accordingly, my definition of orthodoxy should be taken as a proposal rather than an assertion. I would welcome further debate on the topic and would consider the book a success if it stimulates others to refine and advance a better definition. After all, it is not how one defines the word that determines whether or not he is orthodox but what he believes that makes him so.

My reasons for writing on this subject are twofold. First, I am deeply disturbed by the apathy of many Christians towards theology and doctrine. Many believers are seeking experiences but not truth and have little concept of either the importance or relationships between the various doctrines of the Christian faith. Second, I am troubled by the dogmatism of other Christians on secondary and tertiary issues. It is proper to have firm convictions in these areas since there is no such thing as an unimportant biblical truth. But it is terribly improper to alienate other believers who differ on subordinate issues. Hopefully this book will arouse those who are apathetic to take doctrine more seriously while calming those who suspect everyone else of heresy.

I would like to thank Dick Benjamin, Donald H. Carson, Robert G. Clouse, James H. Feeney, Richard B.

Gaffin, Jr., Norman Geisler, and Robert Preus for review-
ing and critiquing the manuscript. I trust that respond-
ing to their comments, both favorable and unfavorable,
made the final product more coherent and edifying. Of
course the contents of the book remain my responsibility alone.

Joel Parkinson
July 27, 1991

Chapter 1

Introduction

What exactly is orthodoxy? The Bible does not use the word "orthodoxy," nor does it give us a clear-cut definition of what it is. The word "orthodoxy" itself means "right opinion" or "correct belief." But what does this entail? Various answers to this question have included the following:

1) The affirmations of the Apostles' Creed,[1]
2) The affirmations of some other confession,[2]
3) The truths about the person and work of Christ,[3]
4) The essentials of the Christian gospel,[4] *DIFF?*
5) The beliefs commonly held by the whole Church,[5]
6) Or even the whole of biblical truth.[6]

Indeed, a whole range of definitions for orthodoxy are possible and each one leads to a different set of truths as a standard for sound Christian doctrine. Generally heresy is presumed to be anything opposite to or contrary to orthodoxy (whatever that is).

The ambiguity surrounding the meaning of orthodoxy and heresy has led to serious problems in the Church. Whenever an overly broad or simplistic view of orthodoxy has been adopted, there has been too much tolerance of serious doctrinal error to the ultimate demise of the church in question. For instance, to espouse "No creed but Christ" and really mean it may ultimately lead to Liberalism.[7] Statements like "No creed but Christ" and "No doctrine but Jesus" might sound spiritual. But in fact they open the door to the "christ" of Jehovah's Witnesses, of Mormons, of Liberalism and of the New Age Movement, which are no christs at all! Is Jesus Christ God? That is a doctrine. Is Christ a man? That is also a doctrine. Did He die for our sins and rise from the dead? These are two more doctrines. Simple assertions such as these are essential to the Christian faith and their denial is fatal to the Church's life and mission.

On the other hand, an overly narrow view of orthodoxy is divisive and repressive. If a church maintains that *all* that it believes is necessary to genuine Christianity,[8] then many ugly consequences result. Churches with *any* differing views are automatically viewed as heretical. Believers are forced into a single mold of belief. All dissenting opinions and contrary questions are silenced. The church becomes entrenched in its views and becomes its own final and infallible authority rather than the Bible. Therefore, an excessively strict definition of orthodoxy is divisive, authoritarian and leads to legalism.

Coming to terms with the meaning of orthodoxy and heresy is especially important for elders who are entrusted with the task of guarding the flock of God from both external and internal threats (Acts 20:28-30). "He must hold firmly to the trustworthy message as it has been taught, so that he can encourage others by sound doctrine and refute those who oppose it" (Titus 1:9). A pastor or elder especially must be convinced of what is essential to the faith and what is not. Otherwise, he may either permit a heresy to grow like a cancer within the body of Christ or needlessly cut off those parts of the body which hold a differing, though not fatal, conviction.

Discerning serious error is similar to a surgeon's diagnosis of a disease in the human body. Gangrene, for instance, is a deadly malady that can be fatal if it is allowed to spread. Consequently, a doctor may decide to amputate an arm or leg to save the victim's life. On the other hand, it would be overreacting (to say the least) to cut off an arm that has a sunburn. In one case, amputation is necessary for survival. In the other it would be sheer stupidity. In both cases a proper diagnosis of the seriousness of the affliction decides the case. So also the Church must diagnose and treat doctrinal error with discernment.

How are we to define orthodoxy objectively? As we have already noted, the Bible gives us no clear definition. One might draw up a list of truths believed to be necessary to orthodoxy (somewhat like a creed), but ultimately some rationale or guiding principle is necessary to determine what truths should be included in such a

FUNCTIONAL
THE GOSPEL

list. It would seem that the best approach is to define orthodoxy in terms of what is essential for man's salvation. Whatever threatens the integrity of man's salvation must be fervently opposed and those who actively teach such things must be shunned. On the other hand, errors that do not endanger the church's existence also may be graciously opposed, yet we should accept those who hold these views into fellowship.

For this book, the following definition of orthodoxy is proposed:

GOOD
SO FAR

BUT PW 4
OF PW 4

> Orthodoxy is that system of beliefs or truths all of which (nothing more and nothing less) is necessary to scripturally, systematically and consistently maintain the basis and content of the true gospel and way of salvation.

In other words, orthodoxy entails those things essential to man's salvation and those biblical doctrines necessary to make salvation possible, coherent and effective. It is a self-sufficient system of truth. Anything less than orthodoxy leaves us with loose ends that a perceptive critic can pull to unravel the fabric of the whole Christian faith. (How many perfectly good socks have been undone by yanking a single loose thread?) However, the things that are not within the scope of orthodoxy are things that can be legitimately debated among believers without jeopardizing Christianity itself.

FACT OF CREATION VS
MANNER OF CREATION

End Notes

1. The Apostles' Creed is an inadequate definition of orthodoxy because it does not say enough. For example, it says that "Jesus Christ...was crucified, dead," but it does not add the all-important fact that He "died *for our sins.*" Moreover, the Creed says nothing about the deity of Christ.

2. Virtually every formal confession of faith is a comprehensive definition of a denomination's doctrine. They include much more than what is essential to Christianity.

3. Although the person and work of Jesus Christ embodies the gospel (1 Cor. 15:1-5), stopping there leaves something to be desired as a definition of orthodoxy. As will be shown later in the essay, too many other factors intertwine with the gospel and are essential to the faith. It would seem, for example, that the early church adopted the Trinity as a test of orthodoxy in opposition to Arianism partly because the issues at stake influenced one's perspective of the gospel and salvation.

4. The essential truths of the gospel are an inadequate measure of orthodoxy for the same reasons that the person and work of Christ are inadequate.

5. It is doubtful that there is much of anything that *all* churches who claim to be Christian believe. Therefore, if we take the common beliefs of the church to mean those things universally held, then we are left with nothing that is orthodox. On the other hand, if by that

which is commonly held by the church we mean that which the majority of the church believes, then majority rule in the church, rather than the Bible, becomes our rule of faith (*contra sola scriptura*); such a transient and subjective approach is unacceptable.

6. If orthodoxy is identified with all biblical truth, then *no one* is orthodox. The Bible speaks on many matters, all of which are debated. At some point, every fallible human being is probably in error in their biblical interpretation.

7. See the superb book by Gordon H. Clark, *Faith and Saving Faith* (Jefferson, Maryland: Trinity Foundation, 1983), p. 49. This book is also available from Presbyterian and Reformed.

8. Exclusive churches include the Roman Catholic church and the United Pentecostal church among others.

Chapter 2

What Is the Gospel?

The first step in defining what is involved in orthodoxy is to define the gospel. Fortunately, the gospel is rather easily defined biblically, unlike the broader term of orthodoxy. In particular, the Apostle Paul defined the gospel in First Corinthians 15.

"Now, brothers, I want to remind you of the gospel I preached to you, which you received and on which you have taken your stand" (1 Cor. 15:1). Here, Paul is introducing the gospel that he preached to the Corinthians and that they received. He is preparing to summarize it in the following verses. But before we consider his description of the gospel, it might be worth noting that he calls it a *gospel*. That is, it is *good news*. The gospel is first of all good and positive. It is secondly news—an account of historical events, not of abstract ideas or myths.

"By this gospel you are saved, if you hold firmly to the word I preached to you. Otherwise, you have believed in vain" (1 Cor. 15:2). By *this* gospel you are saved. There is, after all, only one true gospel (Gal. 1:6-9). *Nothing more* is necessary to believe for salvation, otherwise this gospel could not be said to save. And *nothing less* can be believed, otherwise Paul says the belief is in vain and without effect.

"For what I received I passed on to you as of first importance..." (1 Cor. 15:3a). Paul once again emphasizes the importance of the gospel. It is of *first importance*.[1] Nothing else is more important than what Paul is about to describe. But since the whole gospel is necessary to salvation, none of the things Paul is about to describe is more or less important than the others. They are all equally preeminent.

"...that Christ died for our sins according to the Scriptures, that he was buried, that he was raised on the third day according to the Scriptures, and that he appeared to Peter, and then to the Twelve" (1 Cor. 15:3b-5). Paul identifies three things that are absolutely necessary to the gospel and to our faith. These are: *the person of Christ Himself* (He is both God and man),[2] that *He died for our sins*, and that *He was raised on the third day*. (The further truths of His burial and appearances are not so much necessary to salvation as they are reinforcements and evidences of His physical death and physical resurrection.[3])

All three of these truths are "according to the [Old Testament] Scriptures" (e.g. Is. 9:6, Dan. 9:26, Hos. 6:2-3). All three truths are the common preaching of the apostles (e.g. Acts 2:22-24, 3:15-16, 4:10-12). All three truths are elsewhere identified with the gospel by Paul (e.g. Rom. 1:1-4, 1 Cor. 1:17, 2 Tim. 2:8). Faith in all three truths is necessary for our salvation (e.g. John 8:24, Rom. 3:22-26, 4:24-25).

At this point someone might object that, in verses like John 3:16, all that is required for eternal life is faith in Jesus Christ. In response it must be recognized that faith *in* Jesus Christ entails faith that certain things *about* Him are true. One cannot overcome the world without believing first that Jesus is the Son of God (1 John 5:5). One cannot have God unless he believes that Jesus came in the flesh as a man (2 John 7-9). And we have already seen that believing that Christ died for our sins and rose from the dead is crucial to salvation. Accordingly, when the jailer asked Paul and Silas what he must do to be saved, they answered, "Believe in the Lord Jesus" (Acts 16:31). But they did not leave it at that. They went on and "spoke the word of the Lord to him" (Acts 16:32) in order to explain what it *meant* to believe in Jesus.

So it is true that it is ultimately the person of Jesus Christ in whom we have faith. But to have faith in someone we must first believe certain things about him. For example, I am not very likely to have confidence in my doctor unless I believe that he is knowledgeable in his diagnosis, honest in his prognosis and skillful in his surgical ability. I must believe in his person (knowledge and truthfulness) and work (surgical skill) to entrust myself to his care. Similarly, I must know certain things about Jesus Christ's person and work in order to trust in the true Jesus Christ as my Lord.

The importance of the particular truths of Christ's person, death and resurrection for salvation is clear. The only reason that Christ's death and resurrection count for our salvation is because of who and what He is. Many thousands have died the death of Roman crucifixion and others, like Lazarus (John 11:4) and Tabitha (Acts 9:40), were temporarily raised from the dead. But none of these people can save for none of them were divine or sinless. Furthermore, if Jesus did not die for our sins, then we would still bear the guilt and responsibility for them. And if He was not raised from the dead, then perhaps His atonement was unsuccessful, or is incomplete or He was mistaken in His claims. Together the three truths of the gospel lead us to the true Savior. Separately, they are impotent.

So the gospel consists of the divine-human person, death and resurrection of Jesus Christ. If someone truly believes these three things, then they are saved (1 Cor. 15:2). If one or more of these truths are rejected, then that person is lost.

End Notes

1. Some translate this phrase as "first of all" rather than "of first importance." But even if it refers to what Paul initially preached to the Corinthians, isn't it legitimate to say that it was also what Paul thought was most important?

2. The fact that Christ is God and man is not plainly an aspect of the gospel in First Corinthians 15:1-5. However, it is implicit in the name of "Christ" and is more explicit in Romans 1:1-4.

3. This idea is the conclusion of Ulrich Wilkens in *Resurrection* (Atlanta, Georgia: John Knox Press, 1978), p. 7, and of John Frederick Jansen in *The Resurrection of Jesus Christ in New Testament Theology* (Philadelphia, Pennsylvania: Westminster Press), p. 41.

Chapter 3

What Is the Way of Salvation?

The second step to defining orthodoxy is to define the way of salvation. This question is somewhat different from "What is the gospel?" The gospel is the ground or basis of eternal life, whereas the way of salvation is the personal appropriation of eternal life. The two are quite different things. The gospel is historical and therefore objectively true for all men at all times (1 Cor. 15:3-5). But, only those who receive the gospel subjectively are personally saved and secure salvation (1 Cor. 15:1-2).

Technically, the way of salvation is "justification by grace through faith" in the gospel alone. God freely justifies sinners on the basis of the finished work of Christ and through their faith in this finished work (Rom. 3:22-24). In other words, we are saved by believing the gospel of Jesus Christ's death and resurrection. We do not need to do good works of any kind to get saved (Gal. 2:16, Eph. 2:8-9, 2 Tim. 1:9, Titus 3:4-6). Such good works are merely the product of faith (Rom. 1:5, 14:23, 1 Thess. 1:3, Heb. 11:6) as we are led and renewed by the Holy Spirit (Rom. 8:14, Gal. 5:16, Phil. 2:13, Titus 3:5). Nor do we need to believe anything beyond the truths of First Corinthians 15:3-5 to be saved (1 Cor. 15:2). But we must believe at least this much and believe it firmly.

Of course, we must also repent or perish (Luke 13:3). But, repentance is simply the flip-side of faith. Faith is the certainty of things unseen (Heb. 11:1). So to come to believe something necessarily means a change of mind from what was previously believed. On the other hand, repentance (Greek: *metanoia*) literally means a "change of mind," usually concerning the course of life. Therefore, coming to faith is a change of mind about what is true while repentance is a change of mind concerning our lifestyle. Thus, Paul "declared to both Jews and Greeks that they must turn to God in repentance and have faith in our Lord Jesus" (Acts 20:21). One cannot really turn to God without faith in Jesus, nor can one have faith in Jesus without turning to God. They are two sides of the same coin.[1] Both faith (1 Tim. 1:14, 2 Pet. 1:1) and repentance (Rom. 2:5, 2 Tim. 2:25) are gracious gifts of God. Both faith (Eph. 2:8-9) and repentance (2 Cor. 7:10) necessarily lead to salvation. Both faith (James 2:18) and repentance (Acts 26:20) are proved genuine by good works. The one cannot be separated from the other. To come to genuine faith *is* to repent.

To illustrate the connection and yet the distinction between faith, repentance and their result in good works, consider the stock market. Let's say that somehow you come to believe *with certainty* (i.e., true belief) that the stock market will triple in the next month and that making money on the stock market is good. If you are sure that this situation is the case, then you cannot possibly fail to *decide* to invest the money presently in your savings account in the stock market and then *follow through* with the actual investment. The belief necessitates a decision and leads to the act. So also authentic faith in Jesus Christ accompanies repentance and leads to good works. The three are inseparable but it is only faith (entailing repentance) that brings justification.

The relationship between the gospel and our appropriation of eternal life is beautifully summarized in perhaps the most famous verse of the Bible:

For God so loved the world (God's motivation behind the gospel) *that he gave his one and only Son* (the gospel itself), *that whoever believes in him* (our response to the gospel) *shall not perish but have eternal life* (the result of the gospel).

(John 3:16)

End Notes

1. John Murray wrote that faith and repentance are twin sisters (p. 87) and that they cannot be disentangled (p. 113) in *Redemption: Accomplished and Applied* (Grand Rapids, Michigan: Eerdmans, 1955). See also *Faith and Saving Faith* by Gordon H. Clark (p. 59).

Chapter 4

What Is Orthodoxy?

Having defined the gospel and the way of salvation, we are now prepared to return to the definition of orthodoxy. As previously stated, we will define orthodoxy as the system of beliefs necessary to maintain the basis and essence of the true gospel and way of salvation. Given this definition, it is obvious that the truths entailed in the gospel and in the way of salvation are also entailed in orthodoxy. However, at least seven other doctrines are necessary to systematically support the coherence and validity of the gospel and salvation. These are:

1) The inspiration and inerrancy of the Bible,
2) The Trinity,
3) The virgin birth and incarnation of Christ,
4) The creation of man by God,
5) The sinfulness of man,
6) The judgment of sin by God,

17

7) And the reality of hell as a state of unending torment.

The truths that are essential to the orthodox faith are arranged in Figure 1 to illustrate their interdependence:

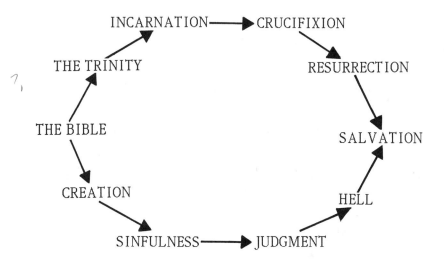

Figure 1 The Interdependence of Orthodox Doctrines

This diagram begins and ends with the Reformation principles of *sola Scriptura* (Scripture alone for doctrine) and *sola fide, sola gratia* (faith alone, grace alone for salvation). The arrangement also shows a logical relationship between the various doctrines. The Bible itself is our starting point because it reveals the other truths and what they mean. For example, it is only through the revelation of Scripture that we can know that God is a triune God (Matt. 28:19). In turn, the incarnation of the Son of God depends upon the Trinity (Luke 1:35), the Son became man in order to die for our sins (1 John 4:10), and Christ died only to be raised again from the dead (Acts 2:24), constituting a finished work that is the basis of salvation.

In the bottom portion of the diagram, it is primarily on biblical grounds that Christians rightly oppose the modern theory of evolution.[1] Since all mankind descended from the one created and fallen man (Rom. 5:12), we are all sinful (Eccl. 7:20). This sinfulness warrants God's judgment that sinners be condemned to hell (Ezek. 18:20, Mark 9:43). How do these truths feed into salvation? Only the double-edged sword of the bad news of judgment with the good news of Jesus brings a sinner to his knees before God. Only when the truths of heaven and hell converge upon the lost will they respond. To offer a man eternal life without confronting him with eternal death is as meaningless as it is cruel to depict his descent into hell without declaring the way of escape.

Now there are clearly doctrinal relationships other than those we have briefly sketched out here. It is the task of systematic theology to explore these relationships. The point here is that each of these truths ultimately depends on each of the others. That is why they are all essential to the Christian faith and compose the tenets of orthodoxy. To deny any one of these facts could have disastrous implications, as shown by the following examination of each of the orthodox doctrines.

The Bible

"All Scripture is God-breathed" (2 Tim. 3:16). It is not that God approved words that originated with men nor that He conveyed ideas to them which they put into their own words. God breathed out[2] the very words of Scripture and *all* of the words in Scripture at that! This means the Bible is word-for-word God's word (Ex. 34:27, Jer. 26:2, John 12:49, 1 Cor. 14:37, Rev. 2:18), and everything that it affirms is without error (Matt. 5:18, Luke 1:34, John 10:35, 17:17, 2 Pet. 1:19).[3]

Consequently, the Bible is sufficient in itself to reveal to us all that we need to know for salvation, teaching and good works (2 Tim. 3:15-17). This revelation is either explicit or, "by good and necessary consequence may be deduced from Scripture."[4] A good algebra textbook, for instance, may not give the answers to every algebra problem. Yet it does fully define the rules and principles by which every algebra problem may be solved. The Bible likewise contains all that we need for our relationship with God even if it does not provide *direct* answers for every problem we face. Since this information is from the mouth of God and without error, it is the final authority on all matters of faith and practice.

These affirmations are necessary to orthodoxy because the truths of the gospel depend upon the truth of the Bible. The Bible defines the gospel and tells us the meaning of the cross and of the resurrection. It tells us who and what Jesus Christ is. Without a God-inspired Bible, we are faced with Scriptures of varying quality from many conflicting sources. Without an inerrant Bible we have no objective criteria for determining what is theologically true. Without a sufficient Bible we would be in the dark about some necessary aspects of what Christianity is all about, what God is like and what He demands of us. Thus, the inspiration, inerrancy and sufficiency of the Bible are essential to orthodoxy, for without them we could have no orthodoxy.

To illustrate the critical place that Scripture has in the faith, let us consider a famous book recently edited by John Hick, entitled *The Myth of God Incarnate*. The contributors to this symposium begin with a denial of Scripture inerrancy.[5] It is then followed by denials of the virgin birth,[6] the incarnation,[7] the substitutionary death of Jesus Christ[8] and His physical resurrection.[9] One could hardly imagine a more complete dismantling of the Christian faith and yet the authors claim to have denied nothing essential to Christianity![10] Now this example does not demonstrate that everyone who denies the inerrancy of Scripture will go all the way down this path of apostasy. But Scripture is the objective truth from which we derive all of our doctrine. Once the Bible itself is questioned, the door is opened to total theological catastrophe.

The Trinity

The Trinity is the next doctrine in the diagram of Figure 1. The doctrine of the Trinity states that there is only one God (John 17:3, 1 Cor. 8:6, 1 Tim. 2:5) consisting of three persons: God the Father, God the Son and God the

Holy Spirit (Matt. 28:19, 2 Cor, 13:14, Eph. 4:4-6). Each of these persons are fully and co-equally God (John 20:17, Rom. 9:5, Acts 5:3-4) and yet they are distinct persons (Mark 1:10-11, John 15:26, Heb. 9:14). Here is not the place to explain or defend this doctrine in detail.[11] But it can be readily shown that the Trinity is essential to the truth of the gospel and salvation.

BUT IT IS A DEDUCTION FROM TRUTHS OF GOSPEL

First of all, Christ's death for our sins is a distinctly trinitarian event. He offered Himself to God the Father through the Holy Spirit (Heb. 9:14). This structure demands the Trinity. It would be senseless to say that Jesus offered Himself to Himself through Himself. Thus the three persons must be distinct. And yet, all three must be God. Only God Himself could save man and fulfill the requirements for such an offering. Only God Himself could receive such an offering and forgive sin. Only God Himself could mediate such an offering.

The incarnation, resurrection and personal salvation are likewise trinitarian events: "The angel answered, 'the *Holy Spirit* will come upon you, and the power of the *Most High* will overshadow you. So the holy one to be born will be called the *Son of God*'" (Luke 1:35, emphasis added). "And if the *Spirit* of *him* who raised *Jesus* from the dead is living in you, *he* who raised *Christ* from the dead will also give life to your mortal bodies through his *Spirit*,who lives in you" (Rom. 8:11, emphasis added). "[God's elect] have been chosen according to the foreknowledge of *God the Father*, through the sanctifying work of the *Spirit*, for obedience to *Jesus Christ* and sprinkling by his blood" (1 Pet. 1:2, emphasis added). So although belief in the Trinity may not be a prerequisite for salvation, the reality of the Trinity is most definitely a prerequisite for the gospel.

To demonstrate the importance of the Trinity, let's consider the correlation between denials of the Trinity and denials of justification by faith. As far as I know, no church or denomination that rejects an aspect of the Trinity holds to justification by faith *alone*. This is undoubtedly because it is recognized (sometimes unconsciously) that justification by faith alone can be maintained only on the basis of Christ's vicarious death on the cross. And this, in turn, can be understood only within a trinitarian framework (recall Heb. 9:14).

For example, Jehovah's Witnesses deny that Jesus Christ and the Holy Spirit are truly God.[12] Only God the Father is true God and the Son and the Holy Spirit are in *necessary* (not voluntary) subordination to Him.[13] On the other hand, Mormons affirm that the Father, the Son and the Holy Spirit are each God, but deny their unity. The Mormons believe in *many* gods, not one.[14] Furthermore, some Liberals recognize that the Father, Son and Spirit are each God, but are merely different modes or manifestations of the same person.[15] When God creates, He is the Father. When God saves, He is the Son. When He sanctifies, He is the Holy Spirit. There is no more threeness in God than there is threeness in "me, myself and I." Finally, United Pentecostals also hold that the three are God, but only one person. But they differ from certain Liberals in that God was once (in the Old Testament) the Father. He then *became* the Son and finally now manifests Himself as the Holy Spirit. God is three only in the sense that a person who was an infant and later grew into a child and then an adult is three. Certainly these non-trinitarian theologies have few similarities between them. However, they are all united in their denials of justification by faith *alone* and, in their own peculiar ways, add some type of good works to the equation.[16]

Again we see how essential the Trinity is to orthodoxy. To believe in the Trinity may not necessarily guarantee sound doctrine elsewhere (for example, Roman Catholics believe in the Trinity but deny justification by grace through faith alone). But to deny the Trinity is virtually a guarantee of fatal error elsewhere. Therefore, the Trinity is an integral part of orthodoxy just as the Bible is. As David wrote, "you have exalted above all things your name [who God is] and your word [what he says]" (Ps. 138:2). Paul committed the Ephesian elders "to God and to the word of his grace" (Acts 20:32). We can do no less in our theological priorities.

The Incarnation

The Lord Jesus Christ is both truly and fully God (John 1:1, Rom. 9:5, Titus 2:13) and truly and fully man (Acts 2:22, 1 Tim. 2:5, 1 John 4:1-2). The union between these two natures is what the doctrine of the incarnation is all about (John 1:1, 14, Rom. 1:3-4, Phil. 2:5-8).[17] The importance of the incarnation should be self-evident. If believing that Jesus Christ is both God and man is necessary to salvation, then clearly the fact that the Son of God became a man is necessary to orthodoxy. Jesus could not be a mediator between God and man (1 Tim. 2:5) without being both. If He was only a man, then His life would have proved that other men like us can potentially save ourselves by good works and human merit. But if He was only God and never became man, then He could not have died a sacrificial death for our sins.

The truth of the incarnation also entails other truths about Jesus Christ. The virgin birth of Jesus Christ tells us *how* God became man (Matt. 1:21, Luke 1:35). The fact that Jesus is God insured His sinless life as a man (2 Cor. 5:21, 1 John 3:5). The fact that He became a man permitted Him to experience and sympathize with our temptations (Matt. 4:1-11, Heb. 4:15). All this is critical to the effectiveness and coherence of our salvation and hence essential to orthodoxy.

The Crucifixion

As part of the gospel, the crucifixion of Jesus Christ is obviously essential to orthodoxy. More specifically, a certain view of the crucifixion is necessary to orthodoxy: *ATONE-MENT* that Christ died *for* our sins. That means He died in our place (1 Pet. 3:18), paid the penalty for our sins (Gal. 3:13), purged sin itself in believers (1 John 1:7), and did so in a way that was compatible with God's righteousness and justice (Rom. 3:25-26).

It is true that Christ gave His life as a ransom (1 Tim. 2:6, Heb 9:15) and was victorious over the devil (Col. 2:15, Heb. 2:14). But the ransom was most certainly not paid to Satan as asserted by the "Ransom Theory" or "Classic Idea" of atonement.[18] In the context of First Timothy 2:6 and Hebrews 9:15, Jesus is the mediator between *God* and man (1 Tim. 2:5) and He offered Himself to *God* (Heb. 9:14). No mention is made of Satan. The term "ransom," only indicates that the sacrifice was costly, not that it was a demonic bribe. Jesus triumphed because He opened the way to God, not because He paid off the devil.

It is also true that Christ's death was the supreme demonstration of God's love for mankind (Rom. 5:8, 1 John 4:9). However, this example of love was a byproduct rather than the main purpose of the crucifixion, contrary to the "Moral Influence Theory" of atonement.[19] Again the context shows that divine love was shown by saving us from God's wrath (Rom. 8:9) through Christ's atoning sacrifice or propitiatory death (1 John 4:10).

Part of the beauty of God's gift in the atonement is that so much is wrapped up in it. Yet to reduce the cross to merely an example of God's love or only a victory over the devil misses the main point. It is like a masterpiece painting. Who can look at Monet's "Rouen Cathedral Main Entrance" and call it a painting of the ground or the sky? Certainly there is ground before the cathedral and sky above it, but it is clearly the imposing cathedral itself which is the subject. Likewise, God's love is the motivation underlying the atonement (John 3:16) and victory over Satan is the result (Heb. 2:14), but these are the foreground and backdrop to the central theme. As J.

Gresham Machen put it, "they are swallowed up in a far greater truth—that Christ died instead of us to present us faultless before the throne of God."[20]

The Resurrection

The resurrection of Jesus is likewise entailed in orthodoxy because it is a part of the gospel. But again we must pause to consider its meaning and significance. In First Corinthians 15:12-19, Paul is quite clear what is at stake in denying the physical resurrection of Jesus Christ. Apart from the resurrection our faith is useless (v. 14), apostolic testimony is false and therefore the Bible erroneous (v. 15), we are still in our sins (v. 17), and our hope is utterly misplaced (v. 19).

Now it is generally recognized that the resurrection vindicated Christ's claims (Acts 2:22-24) and openly declared that He is the Son of God (Rom. 1:3-4). But the resurrection is much more than a Christian evidence. Paul says that apart from Christ's resurrection we are still in our sins! Jesus Christ's resurrection constitutes the cause and guarantee of our conversion (Rom. 6:1-11, Eph. 2:5-6) and future resurrection (1 Cor. 15:20-23, Col. 1:15-18) because we are *united with Him* through faith and by the Holy Spirit.[21] We are justified by Christ's resurrection as much as we are by His death (Rom. 4:25). So it is futile to debate whether the crucifixion or resurrection is more central to Christianity. Eliminate one and the other quickly follows.

Salvation

The way of salvation (previously discussed) is an imperative of orthodoxy because it is the means of personally appropriating the benefits of the gospel. It does not do any good to accept the gospel as true historically if one does not accept it as true personally. It is like saying aspirin will cure a headache and on that basis expect it to remove the pain without actually swallowing the pills.

Yet we must make a further qualification to the gracious gift of redemption: believing the gospel is the *only* way of salvation. This word "only," may offend, but it is necessary to confront, convict and convert. "Jesus answered, 'I am the way and the truth and the life. No one comes to the Father except through me'" (John 14:6). "Salvation is found in no one else, for there is no other name under heaven given to man by which we must be saved" (Acts 4:12). "For there is one God and one mediator between God and man, the man Christ Jesus" (1 Tim. 2:5). To say otherwise is to empty the gospel of all of its power and render Christ's death meaningless. So, "I do not set aside the grace of God, for if righteousness could be gained through the law [or good works, or the mere mercy of God, or through any other means], Christ died for nothing!" (Gal. 2:21).

The Creation of Man

The biblical concept of God's creation of man might appear to be a strange component to orthodoxy. Besides the current popularity of the theory of evolution, such a concept might seem to be remote from the essentials of the gospel. But deep down, man's creation by God is fundamental to the salvation of man for at least three reasons:

1) It is because man was created by God that he is morally responsible to Him (Rom. 9:19-20). Only because God made man does He have an inherent right to make demands on him. Otherwise, His only claim to authority would be some notion of "might makes right," which is not a righteous claim.

2) It is because God first created one couple (Adam and Eve) that we are all in need of salvation. Since Adam fell and we have all descended from him, we are all fallen and sinful (Rom. 5:12-14). But if we cannot trace our ancestry to a single couple, then in theory we are not all *necessarily* sinners and the gospel becomes superfluous.

3) It is because the human race fell as the direct result of one man's sin that because of one man's righteousness we can be saved (Rom. 5:18-19, 1 Cor. 15:22). If Adam was not our singular father, then Christ cannot be our singular Savior.

In short, Adam's creation is the basis for our moral responsibility to God, the cause of our sinfulness before God and the precedent for our reconciliation with God. Man's creation is an orthodox tenet indeed!

I recall an occasion shortly after I was saved when I was witnessing to an atheist friend of mine. He argued that the Bible claims God created the heavens and the earth in six days, but that science has "proved" otherwise. Hence he resolved that the Bible is wrong on the first thing that it teaches. Why then should anything else that it teaches be believed? Other atheists have seized the truth of the second Adam (Romans 5) and argued that evolution makes it impossible for a single Savior (Jesus or anyone else) to redeem mankind. They conclude that the gospel is an impossibility even if there is a God. Now if even atheists recognize the importance of creationism to the Christian faith and exploit it for their purposes, it is time for the Church to do the same and acknowledge that creationism is a central tenet of orthodoxy.

On a conciliatory note, I am willing to grant that those who interpret the six days of creation to be six indefinite ages can remain orthodox[22] even though I believe the biblical evidence is quite to the contrary. The central issues to orthodoxy are creation *ex nihilo* (out of nothing; John 1:3, Col. 1:16, Heb. 11:3) and the literal creation of Adam. Creation out of nothing preserves God's sovereignty by denying the existence of anything independent of the Lord. As we have already seen, Adam's creation preserves the truth of the gospel and opposes any notion of "theistic evolution." But the time frame of Genesis 1 can theoretically be contested without puncturing orthodoxy so long as Adam's appearance on the scene is immediate.

The Sinfulness of Man

The universal sinfulness of man should need little defense as a component of orthodoxy. The gospel is only meaningful and salvation is only necessary if we have sinned. Christ died for *our* sins. Indeed, "If we claim to be without sin, we deceive ourselves and the truth is not in us" (1 John 1:8).

The Judgment of God

Likewise, the fact that God will judge our sins is necessary to orthodoxy. Who cares if we are sinners if God doesn't care? If He will excuse our little white lies and minor infractions, then why bother with all this atonement nonsense? Why go through the charade of incarnation, death and resurrection if there is nothing really at stake? There are no excuses and there are no exceptions. We will all be judged so we all need the Savior that is proclaimed in the gospel.

The Reality of Hell

All men are sinners. We will all be judged. On our own merits we are all worthy of a place in hell. This string of truths is what gives the gospel its force and salvation its value. If there is no hell, if there is no downside to our eternal destiny, if in God's mercy everyone will be redeemed, then when presented with a way to be saved we could hardly be blamed by asking, "Saved from what?" The crucifixion and resurrection would not be acts of divine love and grace. They would not even be looked upon as nice gestures from above. They would be, quite rightly, perceived as impotent and foolish blunders and unnecessary theatrics.

Consider a hero who jumps into a river rushing towards a deadly waterfall. If he dives in to save a young woman who is floundering in the water, then his act is a meaningful act of love and courage. But if the woman is standing safely on the bank and the man throws himself into the rapids to "prove his love" for her, then the feat is only an act of stupidity.[23] The woman's peril or safety makes the difference between heroism and foolishness. So also man's peril decides whether or not the crucified and risen Christ is a Savior or a hopeless romantic. Hell gives heaven its appeal to unbelievers.[24] Hell gives the gospel its urgency to us.

Now there might be legitimate debate over the details about hell. Some understand hell to be a literal place that occupies space while others contend that it is a postmortem state of the soul on a different plane of existence. Some interpret the fire of hell literally while others understand it as metaphorical of some other even more terrible and inexpressible misery. These are questions that are of no consequence *to orthodoxy* as we have defined it. But, it is essential that a Christian affirm the unending conscious torment of the lost after physical death.

Summary of Orthodoxy

Expanding on the diagram (Figure 1) of the relationships of doctrines, the dependence of the gospel and salvation upon the rest of the orthodox faith can be illustrated as in Figure 2.

Denying any of these truths and following those denials to their logical conclusions will ultimately contradict or deflate the truth of the gospel and the one and only way of salvation. Of course, to some extent all biblical doctrines are interrelated. But often these connections are "one way streets." Those truths outside orthodoxy may depend upon some elements of the orthodox faith (the truth of Scripture if nothing else), yet

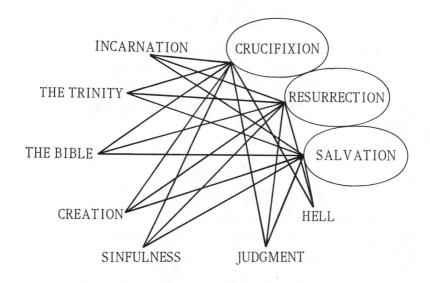

Figure 2 The Dependence of the Gospel on Orthodoxy

orthodoxy does not necessarily depend upon these further truths.

This diagram also vividly illustrates the importance of preaching "theological" as well as "evangelistic" sermons to unbelievers. Sometimes a person's faith in the gospel is hindered by doubt or misconceptions concerning other issues precisely because the truths intertwine. I recently preached a sermon on the Trinity that was a factor in the conversion of a woman who was visiting our church. James Denney once wrote, "If evangelists were our theologians or theologians our evangelists, we should at least be closer to the ideal church."[25] I agree to the extent that all preachers must be grounded in sound theology.

End Notes

1. I say "primarily" because there is substantial evidence for creation and serious scientific problems with evolution. See, for example, Scott M. Huse, *The Collapse of Evolution* (Grand Rapids, Michigan: Baker, 1983).

2. In Second Timothy, 3:16 *Theopneustos* is best rendered "God-breathed" and not "inspired by God."

3. For further discussion, see Stewart Custer, *Does Inspiration Demand Inerrancy?* (Nutley, New Jersey: Craig Press, 1968) and *Inerrancy* edited by Norman Geisler (Grand Rapids, Michigan: Zondervan, 1980).

4. Westminster Confession of Faith, Chapter I.

5. John Hick (ed.), *The Myth of God Incarnate*, (Philadelphia, Pennsylvania: Westminster Press, 1977), pp. ix, 2.

6. Ibid., p. 2.

7. Ibid., pp. ix, 9, 183-184.

8. Ibid., pp. 57-58.

9. Ibid., pp. 59-60.

10. A major theme of the book is supposedly to demonstrate that the incarnation of Jesus Christ can be rejected without denying a central truth of Christianity, (Ibid, pp. 1-10).

11. See *The Trinity* by E. H. Bickersteth (Grand Rapids, Michigan: Kregel Publications, 1955), and *The*

Three Are One by Stuart Olyott (Durham, England: Evangelical Press, 1979).

12. Watch Tower Bible and Tract Society, *Should You Believe in the Trinity?* (Brooklyn, New York, 1989), pp. 15, 20, 23.

13. Ibid., pp. 12, 16, 19.

14. Mormons go so far as to believe that good Mormons can become gods and one day populate their own worlds!

15. Henry Van Dusen is representative of this view of the Trinity with his book, *Spirit, Son and Father*, (New York, New York: Scribner's, 1958), pp. 113, 116, 173-174.

16. Jehovah's Witnesses and Mormons are both known for their insistence on witnessing and other good works to acquire merit with God. Liberals frequently reduce the gospel to a "gospel of love" where all that is required for salvation is the recognition that God loves us and the determination to love other people (a good work). United Pentecostals teach, among other things, that water baptism by immersion and in the name of Jesus only (not the Father, the Son and the Holy Spirit) is a necessary step to salvation.

17. See *Son of Mary, Son of God* by Stuart Olyott (Welwyn, England: Evangelical Press, 1984) and *The Person of Christ* by David F. Wells (Westchester, Illinois: Crossway Books, 1984) for further discussion of the incarnation.

18. See *Christus Victor* by Gustaf Aulen (New York, New York: Macmillan, 1969).

19. This theory is especially popular among Liberals like some of the contributors to *The Myth of God Incarnate* (see note 5).

20. J. Gresham Machen, *Christianity and Liberalism* (Grand Rapids, Michigan: Eerdmans, 1923, 1990), p. 119.

21. For an excellent discussion of how central Christ's resurrection is to the Christian faith, see *Resurrection and Redemption*, by Richard B. Gaffin, Jr. (Phillipsburg, New Jersey: Presbyterian and Reformed, 1978).

22. Two orthodox writers who hold this view are Edward J. Young, *In the Beginning*, (Carlisle, Pennsylvania: Banner of Truth, 1976), p. 43, and J. Rodman Williams, *Renewal Theology* (Grand Rapids, Michigan: Zondervan, 1988), Volume I, p. 108. Both men affirm creation *ex nihilo* and deny evolution.

23. I borrowed the seed thought for this illustration from Leon Morris, *The Cross of Christ*, (Grand Rapids, Michigan: Eerdmans, 1988), p. 21.

24. Of course, the presence of God is what gives Heaven its appeal to believers, but unbelievers have no meaningful knowledge of our relationship to Him and cannot be expected to have this appeal as their initial motive for seeking the truth.

25. James Denney, *The Death of Christ* (New Canaan, Connecticut, Keats Publishing, 1981), preface.

Chapter 5

What Is Heresy?

One biblical sense of heresy (Greek: *hairesis*) is neutral and simply means a party or sect such as the Sadducees (Acts 5:17), Pharisees (Acts 26:5) or Christians (Acts 28:14). But we are interested in the negative sense in which heresy means a dangerous doctrinal error. As Peter wrote, "They will secretly introduce destructive heresies, even denying the sovereign Lord who bought them—bringing swift destruction on themselves" (2 Pet. 2:1). So this heresy is secret in that its proponents never announce it as heresy. It may *even* deny the Lord, showing that this heresy is not limited to such a denial. It finally brings destruction upon its proponents, showing its seriousness.

Having already defined and described orthodoxy, we must now attempt to ascertain what this heresy is. First, a distinction should be noted between that which is unorthodox and that which is heretical. An *unorthodox* doctrine is any belief that is either an outright denial or contradiction of orthodoxy as the word *unorthodox* implies, or a false intrusion of a doctrinal issue into the realm of orthodoxy. Surely to deny or distort any of the truths already discussed would have serious implications. But to further impose any unnecessary factors into the economy of salvation is also very dangerous. A few examples might be instructive and will follow shortly.

On the other hand, a *heretical* doctrine is an unorthodox belief that is actively or publicly promoted in the church. Recall that in Second Peter 2:1 false teachers will *introduce* destructive heresies and that the word "heresy," means a party, sect or faction with a certain system of teaching. So also, Paul condemned those who *preached* a Judaizing gospel (Gal. 1:8-9), not those who merely embraced it. For the latter, Paul himself could wish that he was cursed in their place (Rom. 9:1-3)! Therefore it seems that the teaching of unorthodox doctrines is heretical, not necessarily their adherence.

Now for some examples. Clearly our definition of orthodoxy tolerates different views of water baptism, so long as they do not interfere with the orthodox truths themselves. A Presbyterian can sprinkle infants and a Baptist can immerse believers and both can be genuine and devout Christians. Neither should regard the other as a heretic. Both should regard their differences as a "family disagreement." However, when water baptism is made into a prerequisite for salvation, then one begins to tamper with the orthodox faith.[1] In effect, it denies justification by faith alone and the sufficiency of Christ's

40

death and resurrection. Such an error is most serious and must be avoided in the church.

One might also remain true to the faith as either a non-charismatic or as a charismatic. One's views on spiritual gifts and the like do not necessarily affect one's orthodoxy. Again, Christians on both sides of the issue should accept each other as genuine believers because they both embrace the same faith. Such openness does not mean that we jettison our convictions. It does mean that saints who disagree can fellowship and dialogue together. But woe to him who teaches that a second act of grace and the attendant speaking in tongues is a necessary sign of salvation! Such a teaching would once again be an intrusion into the sacred territory of salvation. And woe to him who places the modern gift of prophecy alongside the Scriptures as infallible and binding.[2] That denies the sufficiency and final authority of the Bible. The church must reject these extremes as divisive and heretical.

These examples could be multiplied. We should tolerate different forms of government in other churches (though only one might be biblically right) within the framework of orthodoxy. But when the church assumes a mediatorial role (as is the case with Roman Catholicism) watch out! There is only one mediator between God and man (1 Tim. 2:5) and all other claimants are heretical. Many schools of thought on eschatology (end times) are tolerable. But when the system begins to warp the one and only way of salvation, even one's end times doctrine can be heretical.[3]

End Notes

1. See, for example, *Baptism: A Biblical Study* by Jack Cottrell (Joplin, Missouri: College Press, 1989). The whole thesis of this book is that a person cannot be saved without being water baptized.

2. Excellent and balanced treatments of contemporary prophecy are given by D.A. Carson in *Showing the Spirit* (Grand Rapids, Michigan: Baker, 1987) and Wayne Grudem in *The Gift of Prophecy in the New Testament and Today* (Westchester, Illinois: Crossway Books, 1988).

3. In *Signs of His Coming* (Minneapolis, Minnesota: Bethany House, 1962), Arthur Bloomfield teaches that during a seven year tribulation people will "receive a special kingdom because of what they did," not because of any conscious faith (p. 149). He further asserts that those people who are alive at that time will be "judged by their works" without regard to their faith (p. 153).

Chapter 6

Some Practical Considerations

The term "heresy" has certain negative connotations that are "hang-overs" from the dark ages. Certainly a heresy is a serious error that must be dealt with effectively. But that does not mean we must put heretics through an "inquisition" and burn them at the stake! Accordingly, we should keep some practical implications in mind as we contend with doctrinal error.

(1)*Orthodoxy does not deny the merit of other doctrines.* It is not that issues besides those of orthodoxy have no value. Indeed, anything addressed by the Bible is of great importance. It is simply that they are not of *critical* value to one's eternal destiny. No individual or church should renounce personal convictions for the sake of an artificial unity. Yet there can be both unity and diversity within the framework of orthodoxy (see

Romans 14). All too often peripheral differences cause us to exclude other Christians from fellowship when, instead, we should capitalize on our similarities, establish lines of communication and attempt to draw them over to our viewpoint. We can also cooperate in the work of evangelism if we embrace the same faith. In spite of their differences, orthodox Christians from many denominations and viewpoints can together "contend for the faith that was once for all entrusted to the saints" (Jude 3).

(2)*Unorthodox views can exist within genuine Christianity.* If believing the gospel is sufficient for salvation and if orthodoxy entails more than the simple gospel, then it follows that genuine Christians can believe unorthodox doctrines. Such cases are often the result of a "blessed inconsistency" where they have not recognized the logical implications of their position as opposed to the gospel. However, this situation is usually "unstable."[1] If the unorthodox belief controls, then ultimately the gospel itself may be denied.[2] If faith in the gospel controls, then ultimately the unorthodox belief will be challenged and swept away.

(3)*Virtually every new believer holds unorthodox views.* Again, believing the gospel brings salvation. But it may take further instruction to convince a new Christian of other orthodox truths. (I initially had trouble with the Trinity and creationism after my conversion from agnosticism until the case for these truths were presented to me clearly and convincingly.) At this point excommunication should *not* be threatened! Ignorant new believers pose little threat to the rest of the congregation. They have neither the command of Scripture nor the convincing power of maturity to lead "old timers" astray. They also have not established enough new relationships in the church for excommunication to be meaningful to them. We cannot go around cutting off every warped branch before it is even grafted into the tree!

(4)*Unorthodox beliefs should be judged in proportion to their intensity.* The intensity of an unorthodox conviction may fall into one of three categories that require varying degrees of urgency and severity in its correction or censure:

i) A TENTATIVE OPINION. Often a person believes something that is unorthodox only temporarily. Once the opposing views are presented or the implications considered, the person quickly becomes open to a change of opinion. The belief has not become acute and the person is teachable. Gentle but firm correction and instruction is appropriate (2 Tim. 4:2-4).

ii) AN ENTRENCHED CONVICTION. At this point the individual may be thoroughly convinced that the belief is true without any indication that he is willing to reconsider his position. The person is unteachable but he has not taken the step of letting the error dominate the rest of his doctrine. This intensity level warrants a clear warning to the person not to spread the teaching. Violations merit the person's excommunication on the grounds of heresy (Rom. 16:17-19, Titus 3:10-11, 2 John 9).

iii) A GUIDING PRINCIPLE. This level goes beyond the entrenched position and actually carries the conviction out to its logical conclusions. The individual recognizes the consequences of his unorthodox belief and begins to deny other truths of the faith on that basis. It is the most serious stage of error that ultimately leads to a denial of the gospel itself. This case also requires warnings of excommunication on heretical grounds and an urgent appeal to repent. Let heresy like this be anathema (Gal. 1:8-9)!

(5)*It is not necessary to call someone a heretic.* Given the definition of heresy and the previous three considerations, it would be very unwise to throw the term "heretic" around freely. Those who keep their views to themselves are merely unorthodox and need further instruction. To call them heretical might offend them and actually wreck any opportunity of correcting the error. Those who publicly contradict orthodoxy are heretical, but the label of heretic may again be counterproductive in the initial phase of confrontation. There might be times when we publicly identify particular heretics for excommunication. But that is a last resort after all attempts at reconciliation with the truth have failed (cf Matt. 18:15-17).

(6)*Heresy is usually sincere.* To say that someone holds an unorthodox or heretical viewpoint does not malign the character of the individual. Some heretics are men of integrity.

(7)*Heresy can be conservative.* To say that someone holds a heretical view does not necessarily mean that they are a died-in-the-wool Liberal. Heresy can spring from rigid, but erroneous, interpretation of God's infallible word as well as from loose explanations of a Bible perceived as flawed throughout.

End Notes

1. In *The Virgin Birth of Christ* (Grand Rapids, Michigan: Baker, 1965), J. Gresham Machen wrote that, "though it is true, though theoretically a man can believe in the resurrection, for example, without believing in the virgin birth, yet such a halfway conviction is not likely to endure ... Remove the part, and the whole becomes harder and not easier to accept" (pp. 396-397).

2. This is a major concern of Harold Lindsell in *The Battle for the Bible* (Grand Rapids, Michigan: Zondervan), 1976. He argues that those evangelical Christians who now accpet errors in the Bible are opening the door to inevitable denial of the gospel in future generations (pp. 142-143, 159).

Chapter 7

Conclusions

The proposed definition of orthodoxy has led to a definite system of doctrines that embody the essentials of the Christian faith as illustrated in Figures 1 and 2. This "grid" helps to draw a tangible line between orthodoxy and heresy. Outside this framework we are dealing with deadly error. Within it we can work towards genuine Christian unity without the emotionalism of crying, "Heretic!" every time someone disagrees with us.

More importantly, this definition provides an objective *principle* for determining what is and what is not heretical. Clearly this brief book does not give a detailed analysis of every orthodox tenet.[1] Nor does it attempt to anticipate every conceivable heretical threat. (In fact, I have omitted discussion of some rather obscure heresies that I have encountered for the sake of space). Yet equipped with this principle, any astute Christian can assess "every wind of doctrine" for its compatibility with the orthodox faith.

Of course, everything that has been said herein concerns how we deal with doctrinal differences within the congregation and with other churches. But a higher standard must be set for leaders within a particular church. It is both biblically correct and practically necessary to demand a high degree of doctrinal unity among the pastor and elders who govern a local church. They must agree on more than basic orthodoxy so they teach with one voice, counsel with one mind and lead with one purpose.

End Notes

1. For example, Christ's session at the right hand of the Father is implied by His resurrection; our regeneration and sanctification are entailed in salvation; God's sovereignty and providence are wrapped up in creation.

Discussion Questions

1) What truths *must* a person believe in order to be a genuine Christian?

2) If we are justified by grace through faith *alone*, then how can repentance be necessary for salvation?

3) In your own words, what exactly is orthodoxy? Why is it important to have a clear definition of it?

4) What do you think are the biblical distinctions between the gospel, the faith and the truth?

5) What role does the Bible's inspiration play in orthodoxy? Its inerrancy? Its sufficiency?

6) Why should such a "complicated" doctrine as the Trinity be essential to the orthodox faith?

7) What are some of the ways that the truth of the incarnation could be denied? How and why are they heretical?

8) How do God's justice, love and victory relate to each other in the crucifixion of Jesus Christ?

9) How does the theory of evolution undermine our only hope for salvation?

10) What characteristics must doctrinal error have in order to be considered heretical?

11) If you were an elder, how would you handle a new believer that embraced an unorthodox doctrine?

12) If you were an elder, how would you deal with a member of your church who taught something unorthodox?